Step by Step

The Story of a Ladybug

It Starts with an Egg

Lisa Owings

Lerner Publications ◆ Minneapolis

Lerner Publications Company
An imprint of Lerner Publishing Group, Inc.
241 First Avenue North
Minneapolis, MN 55401 USA

For reading levels and more information, look up this title at www.lernerbooks.com.

Image credits: B.Forenius/Shutterstock.com, p. 3; Brett Hondow/Shutterstock.com, p. 5; SweetCrisis/Shutterstock.com, pp. 7, 23 (top left); Andrew Palmer/Alamy Stock Photo, p. 9, 23 ; David Long/EyeEm/Getty Images, p. 11; Brett_Hondow/Getty Images, pp. 13, 23 (bottom right); akova/Getty Images, pp. 15, 23 (bottom left); Pavel Sporish/Getty Images, p. 17; kororokerokero/Getty Images, p. 19; Savas Sener/Getty Images, p. 21; Fernando Trabanco Fotografía/Getty Images, p. 22.

Cover: irin-k/Shutterstock.com (ladybug), SweetCrisis/Shutterstock.com (ladybug eggs).

Main body text set in Mikado a Medium.
Typeface provided by HVD Fonts.

Photo Editor: Brianna Kaiser
Lerner team: Sue Marquis

Library of Congress Cataloging-in-Publication Data

Names: Owings, Lisa, author.
Title: The story of a ladybug: it starts with an egg / Lisa Owings.
Description: Minneapolis : Lerner Publications, [2022] | Series: Step by step | Includes bibliographical references and index. | Audience: Ages 4–8 | Audience: Grades K–1 | Summary: "Discover how a tiny egg becomes the recognizable ladybug. Engaging photos offer a close-up look at each step in the life cycle"—Provided by publisher.
Identifiers: LCCN 2021000085 (print) | LCCN 2021000086 (ebook) | ISBN 9781728428253 (library binding) | ISBN 9781728431642 (paperback) | ISBN 9781728430898 (ebook)
Subjects: LCSH: Ladybugs—Life cycles—Juvenile literature.
Classification: LCC QL596.C65 O955 2021 (print) | LCC QL596.C65 (ebook) | DDC 595.76/9—dc23

LC record available at https://lccn.loc.gov/2021000085
LC ebook record available at https://lccn.loc.gov/2021000086

Manufactured in the United States of America
1-49362-49466-3/25/2021

I like ladybugs.
How do they grow?

First, a ladybug finds a place for her eggs.

She lays her eggs in a cluster.

Soon the eggs hatch into larvae.

Each larva eats
the food around it.

Then the larva grows and sheds its skin.

Next, the larva
becomes a pupa.

The pupa's body changes shape.

Finally, the adult
ladybug emerges.

Look, a ladybug!

The new ladybug
helps to keep
away pests.

Picture Glossary

egg

larvae

pupa

shed

Learn More

Kenney, Karen Latchana. *Life Cycle of a Ladybug*. Minneapolis: Pogo, 2019.

Neuenfeldt, Elizabeth. *Ladybug*. Minneapolis: Bellwether, 2021.

Zemlicka, Shannon. *The Story of a Butterfly: It Starts with a Caterpillar*. Minneapolis: Lerner Publications, 2021.

Index

adult, 18

egg, 4, 6, 8

ladybug, 3, 4, 18, 20, 22

larva, 8, 10, 12, 14

pupa, 14, 16